Liturgical Entanglements

Liturgical Entanglements

David Russell Mosley

RESOURCE *Publications* · Eugene, Oregon

LITURGICAL ENTANGLEMENS

Resource Publications
An Imprint of Wipf and Stock Publishers
199 W. 8th Ave., Suite 3
Eugene, OR 97401

www.wipfandstock.com

PAPERBACK ISBN: 978-1-6667-3700-4
HARDCOVER ISBN: 978-1-6667-9602-5
EBOOK ISBN: 978-1-6667-9603-2

JANUARY 21, 2022 10:41 AM

The following poems first appeared in *Macrina Magazine*: "Jacob's Ladder," "The Milky Way," "The Holy Fool," "Ekstasis." "The Stations of the Cross" and "Notre Dame" first appeared in *The Imaginative Conservative*. "Transfiguration" first appeared in *The Green Man* published by Resource Publications. "Liturgical Entanglement" first appeared in *Grand Little Things*.

To my wife, Lauren, and my sons, Theodore and Edwyn
who have followed me into the strange complexities of
the Church Year.

Just as the natural life also grows by means of large cycles of time, made up of many days, so does our Christian life. The liturgy, then, takes the natural year, the cycle of human life which is in harmony with the rhythm of the cosmos, and presents the great phases of the Mystery which we are to undergo throughout the year's recurring days, while, in the celebration of the Eucharist, it transfigures each of these days.

—LOUIS BOUYER, *LIFE AND LITURGY*

Contents

LENT

TRIDUUM

EASTER

ORDINARY TIME

Stations of the Cross

The Planets

Mysteries of the Rosary

Glorious Mysteries

APOSTLES' CREED

Benediction

Preface

I LOVE THE CHURCH CALENDAR. Every year, we go through a kind of non-identical repetition (to borrow a phrase from Kierkegaard). Christmas comes again, but this one is not exactly the same as the one before. Time moves in a spiral in the Church year. It moves forward, yes, but always passes over those key moments again and again. It is a deposit of heaven, a commingling of time and eternity. This is one of the reasons I became Catholic, to live the Church Calendar more fully. So, I've long wanted to write something dealing with it. And that is ultimately where this book in your hands came from.

This book began as an idea several years ago. I was sitting at a teacher training event, bored, and started writing poems reflecting on the Luminous Mysteries of the Rosary. But the whole idea stopped there. Over the rest of that year, I tried to come back to it, but couldn't. Then the pandemic hit. And while bad for the world, it did mean more time to write. But still, I struggled to put together a coherent idea. By Easter Vacation of 2021, however, I was hit by a flurry of inspiration, and composed many of these poems that week. These poems, therefore, bear the mark of the pandemic, of lock downs, and the necessity to practice holiness in the home.

And so I present these poems to you. Seamus Heaney wrote about an old monk hearing his confession in his poem "Station Island XI" telling him to "read poems as prayers." These poems are offered to all of you as just that, prayers. There is no need to read these only during the appropriate season. This book, I hope, can be enjoyed and used at any time. But I do hope that you find many of these poems helpful in your prayer life throughout the Church Year.

May the God who entered into time and joined it to his eternity be with you all.

Sincerely yours,
David Russell Mosley
Feast of St. Nicholas 2021

Acknowledgements

I WANT TO THANK the many friends and family who helped me produce this work of poetry. Mark Forrester, Anne Michelle Carpenter, and Jacob Liyeff were all instrumental in helping me in the drafting stages of this book. I am also immensely grateful to my long-suffering wife for putting up with a husband who decided to turn poet in his thirties.

Introit

"Liturgical Entanglement"

Time has been entangled with the eternal,
Spiralling from Winter into Spring,
And even from the pains of Lent, it brings
Us into Easter, green and vernal.
It has spun me, bound me, turned me all
From individual moments moving
To an eternal now, a present that sings
The past, the present, the future as one in all.
Then the bells ring, the incense clears, the present
Moves again with the ticking of the clock,
It brings me back to myself from beyond the stars.
Once caught in liturgical entanglement
I cannot allow moving time to block
The holy song of the nine heavenly choirs.

Advent

"How Long?"

How long, O Lord, must we wait for your return?
How long until you answer the cries of your people?
We cast our eyes up where the temple steeple
Once stood tall, but now in fire burns.
Just like the leaves in Autumn, our lives are turned
From life to death as part of your deep will
Which we cannot fathom except as our feet well
Traveled lead to the exiled home we earned.
The golden gates of David's city are locked
And the key which will unlock them has been hidden,
But still, the psalms are written on our hearts
Calling forth the Man of Sorrows, bidden
To unlock the Gates of Heaven, his holy part.

"When"

Forty years spent wandering in the desert
Wondering when we'd find the Promised Land.
Returned from exile, our home is now in hand,
From hidden places we dig up our buried treasures.
We return to life, to fasts, to feasts, to pleasure.
We strike the harp and make a merry band,
Praising the God who sought us beyond all measure.
But when will Jesse's root return to flower?
When will the once and future King return?
And when will David come to dwell among us,
Who will overthrow this worldly power,
The adversary waiting for us to burn?
When will the King of Glory come before us?

"Fiat"

It seems an unreal lifetime since the day
I said, "I am the Handmaid of the Lord,"
My "Let it be," a pun, a creation play
On words I did not know, the Roman sword
Still kept me from this language of the West.
But with my *fiat* came a little baby
Whose constant kicking leaves me little rest
As he grows inside my womb, no doubts, no, "maybe
The Lord is playing some awful game with me."
I knew the risks, but took them all the same;
So now I wait, longing desperately to see
The baby boy who will set the world aflame.
For the fires of God's Love burn bright in him
And he will be the Sun that that never dims.

"Shortening"

The light is growing less, the days are shorter,
My candles burn a little longer every night.
I pour myself a drink, an ink-black porter,
And contemplate this shifting in the light.
What does it mean, for those of us in the North,
That God was born a man on the darkest day?
And what about those in the South? They search
For the Christ-child born as Summer begins to play.
North or South or East or West, the World
Prepares for the little Boy we wait to see.
Creation's groans rise up like incense swirled,
Making patterns that set the captive free,
But only if we have the eyes to find
The deeper meaning around the Earth entwined.

"Fallowing"

Fallowing, the leaves turn yellow, gold,
And red, before they all fall to the ground dead.
What do they know, what is it that makes them so bold
To mock the death they're headed to instead
Of fearing it as I have come to do?
Perhaps they know the end for which they're made,
An end that gives them hope to hold on to,
A hope for which their playful spirits prayed.
Perhaps they know the end is not the end,
This death will be transfigured into new life.
And as they fall throughout the air they send
A song of hope, an end to all our strife.
I watch the leaves fall through my window panes,
Wondering what it is in death I gain.

"First Snow"

Winter has not yet arrived, but the first flakes of snow
Begin to fall, blanketing the leaves that fell,
Preparing the ground, preparing new life to grow.
Crystalizing patterns, which move and swell
With the wind, are contained within every flake,
Each one unique, a small world unto itself.
But I cannot see the beauty for which I ache,
Not with naked eyes can I see its wealth.
Beneath this beautiful blanket, more beauty awaits,
In a few months, snowdrops will burst up from the ground,
Rising up like heroes, putting death in its place,
Their greening life from death a new song which resounds.
These snowflakes are a deposit of what is to come,
And I wait with them for the One who will make this home.

"Advent Wreath"

We light another candle on the wreath,
An evergreen bough we brought into our home
Bedecked with candles, purple, white, and pink.
They bring a holy light into the gloam.
As the darkness keeps on creeping into my soul,
These little lights bring stabs of hope and joy.
Though broken down, they begin to make me whole
As I watch them burn and wait for the coming boy.
Mary and Joseph knew dark days, I know,
For God had called them into his radical plan.
But they surrendered, and so must I, to his flow,
That flow of grace poured out from the God-made-man.
So here I sit and watch the flames rise up,
And take another sip from my steaming cup.

Christmas

"Christmas Day"

The celestial choirs, the stars, in heaven sang
As in the cave the baby and his mother
Cried. One with life, the other with joy rang
Out the bells of peace on Earth for brother
Sister, father, mother, for all those waiting,
Waiting for the coming of God with us.
No imperial office, no stockmarket trading,
This little boy would have to take the bus.
He came with celestial signs of his magnificence
But choose a low-class family for his own.
He came to show us that despite our intransigence
He wants us with him on his heavenly throne.
God took on flesh, took on humanity
To raise us up to his divinity.

"Flight to Egypt"

In the moonlit night he leads them on,
The Holy Mother and her still young child.
He knows that he may lead them to the wild
And lonely places of the world. "Be gone,"
The Angel said, and so before the dawn
They left. Perhaps the infant Jesus smiled
And cooed and laughed as the Moon and stars compiled
Their holy song. Perhaps the ocean was calm.
But Rachel wailed and weeped for children lost,
And Herod, like our sin, raged on, and Death
Seemed to hold all in its sway. The Fall
Remained in place. But Egypt leads to the Cross,
To rocks and stones that call out without breath.
But while they walk the stars sound their silent call.

"The Holly and the Ivy"

Why do we look to the holly and the ivy,
The red and green so vibrant in the snow?
What do we learn when we consider them wisely?
What can they teach us that we need to know?
Winter always seems a time of sleep
And sleep is a reminder that we die.
Do these waking plants have a vigil to keep?
Or are they simply standing idly by
Watching everything else succumb to death
While they, the winners, survive the icy cold?
Perhaps I've lost my mind and there's nothing left
But phantoms dancing in a world grown old.
Or perhaps creation is a book,
One we can read if we know where to look.

"Church Bells"

What happened to the bells that used to sing,
The tolling music for rich and poor alike?
They raised songs that taught us time can sing,
And not just march along with a lonely tick.
They used to sing for marriage, for life, for death;
They sang to call the people to their prayers.
And most they rang to sing the Savior's birth,
When shepherds walked beneath angels in the air.
These bells they tolled, they tolled for eternity
Was intermingling with sequential time.
They signaled in the Earth a new viridity
As humanity was united to the divine.
We have neglected the music of the poor,
But we can find it through the stable door.

"Shuttered"

Snow is falling and the days are shorter;
Ice is clinging to our roofs and gutters.
Most people stay inside, everything is shuttered,
Waiting for when the weather will be warmer.
I gather with my friends and family, a harbor,
A haven of peace amidst the snowy flutter.
As we pass the tea and toast with plenty of butter
We sing and laugh, the fire growing colder.
But have we shuttered up our hearts to the poor?
Built our haven with walls that close them out?
And glut ourselves on food we should be sharing?
Remember Joseph knocking at the door,
Remember Mary's grace and lack of doubt
And open up your door for those who need caring.

"Christmas Tree"

The forest waits in furtive anticipation
For the greening of the church and home to start.
The coming Savior brings hope for all creation,
Creation laboring with a mother's heart
To be made new and taken into heaven,
That other space which occupies our own,
Which sometimes can be seen when we are given
The grace to see the heavenly light that shone
On the first day when God had called it into being.
But until the coming Christ appears
We must go on never fully seeing
The trees who clap their hands or the mountain's cheers.
But still we take them in and take them home
Until our verdant Savior finally comes.

"Epiphany"

Show me the New Wine giver, o Blessed Mother,
So I may wash in the water become good wine.
Take me, Unwithered Rose, to see my brother
Whose birth was foretold by a magnificent star that shined
To light the path for those with eyes to see.
The Creator coos amidst the cosmic brilliance
As wizards bring him gifts both precious and holy,
And you see your boy shine with the radiance
Of your God made visible for a moment.
So show me the God-made-man who has appeared,
Whose epiphany will leave the veil torn, rent,
And by every kind of people will be revered.
For he may have come as such a little one,
But he wants to make us into himself, the Son.

Lent

"Ash Wednesday"

The Love that moves the sun and other stars
Now moves me to my end and to my death.
It moves my lungs to take their final breath.
Fasting, weeping, mourning, sighing are
Not able to do me good. Just like Macbeth,
My sins are my undoing. There is nothing left,
No prayer to save my soul, to remove these scars.
But then, the ashes touch my head, and I
Am brought to life. I can return with heart
Made clean by the joy of the Lord born in a stall,
Whose unending love makes sin and darkness die.
But I must repent, give myself, every part.
For God will have me whole, or not at all.

"Quarantine"

Trapped inside our homes we wait in fear,
Wondering what new plague will come,
What fresh hell will come into our homes.
And from a distance we wail and weep our tears.
We cannot find our star by which to steer.
We drift in isolation all alone,
Alone on a sea of quarantine, a tomb,
A cell, where we cannot see, cannot hear.
And yet in this, our social distancing
We have a chance to grow together as one,
As one with Christ and one as family.
Our inward journey must also outwardly sing
Like monks we must enchant a single tone,
And sing to God our cosmic melody.

"Notre Dame"

From arches old, the fires enfold the spire.
The holy relics, art, and host were saved.
The stellar ceiling now reveals the graven
Sky. The circling stars shine through the fire.
Parisians gather to pray and vent their ire,
Grieving loss of culture, loss of faith.
The beads all clinking as they pray *Ave*
Maria. Lady, from the ash and mire
Renew the Church, renew our faith, but first
Teach us to weep when things are gone and remind
Us life is fleeting fast, and we to ash
Will soon return. But while we live we thirst
For justice, truth, and beauty. Fires of mind
Give way to prayer, and from the wreckage, the Cross.

"Peniel"

I've come to wrestle with you again, O Lord,
I've come to see our fight through to the end.
I won't let you go until I have your Word,
Until you've turned me from enemy to friend.
I am beset by demons and temptations,
Like Anthony who lived the hermit's life,
But unlike him I cannot win the commendation,
My struggle leaves me without the will to fight.
But you've come down to fight with me, O God,
And in your presence demons take their flight.
You fight with me because your are my God,
And you bless me through my struggle with your might.
You come to me in every place I dwell,
And so I name each place Blessed Peniel.

"The River"

Plant me by your holy river, o Lord,
The river that flows from the temple of your heart.
Breathe me out like your Son, the Word,
And plant me at the end which is the start
Of my new life in you, new life and new growth
Feeding on the Word, sweeter than honey.
Between the blood and water, I take them both
And drink them in till I am overrunning
With a joy that has made its way through sadness,
A joy that has seen death and overcome it.
This joy in me, it branches into gladness,
It takes the darkness in and undoes it.
But I am not a tree and so can move,
And deny myself my sustenance, your love.

"The Robe"

Lift me up out of the mud and mire,
And bring me into your eternal glory.
Set me in the blaze, the refiner's fire;
Mine me from the sins which are my quarry.
In oceans I have sunk into the depths,
And lost my way in caverns in the mountains.
In dark woods, I lost my sense of right and left,
And in the desert, I drank from the false fountain.
So now I'm stuck in the swamp of sin and darkness,
Waiting on the road to Jericho,
Waiting for the end to all this starkness,
This sense that death will deal its final blow.
So lift me up before I sink too deep
And wrap me in the robe that's mine to keep.

"Confession"

Lay your hands on me, O Lord, and heal me.
Root out the rocks of vice in the soil of my soul.
Cure my cataracts so I may see,
Bring me to my end and make me whole.
The poison flows so quickly in my veins;
I feel it spreading from my sinner's heart.
Like a wicked, unholy habit, it trains
Me to lie, to follow the vicious part.
Take me out of this abysmal wood,
Carry me up to the peak of your Mountain of Light.
I cannot bring myself up or achieve the good
Which you desire for me and which is right.
Breathe me into life and make me new.
Bring me to your home to live with you.

Triduum

"Maundy Thursday"

He came to give us a different kind of life,
But first he had to give a new commandment.
He showed us power doesn't lay in might,
But in one who's dressed in humble habiliment.
His mother said that God will exalt the lowly,
And so he knelt to wash our sin-stained feet.
He lifted up the bread and wine made holy
Before he turned our death into something sweet.
"A new command I give to you," he said,
"That you, my little children, will love each other."
He gave us the simple gifts of wine and bread
So we might be joined to him as sisters and brothers.
He humbled himself to overcome our loss
As he was raised up on the bloody cross.

"Good Friday"

When he was raised up on the bloody cross,
He took on the wage of sin, our wage of death.
The Sky went black because the Light seemed lost,
As Jesus gasped his final, dying breath.
This is the love he commanded us to show,
A love that only seeks the other's good,
A love that causes the Spirit's Wind to blow
And changes bread and wine to spiritual food.
Now I must learn to love just as he did,
And walk upon my own dolorous way.
I have in me a light that should not be hid,
It is my role in life, the Gospel play.
But he was still descending down beyond;
He had to go to the lands without a sun.

"Holy Saturday"

He went down to the lands without a sun
To make his final gospel proclamation.
The devil thought his victory had come;
He didn't understand the plan of salvation.
Death could not contain the One who Is,
And lost so many captives he thought he'd gained.
Hell was harrowed, he destroyed the city of Dis
And so the sting of Death was thus contained.
By dying Christ has built for us a bridge,
A road that no longer leads us straight to Hell,
A road that leads us far away from the edge
Through a different kind of fire that makes all things well.
But still we had to wait for another sunrise
For him to give us a different kind of life.

Easter

"Arise!"

Arise! Arise and meet the risen One.
The Sun is dawning on the newest day.
Death has lost, the devil has not won,
The dead seed is now a tree come out to play.
The week has been re-written and now ends
On the day God said, "Let there be Light."
The Light has been unveiled and eternally sends
The radiance of Joy to those lost in the night.
The first is now the eighth, eternal present,
And its Light shall never be put out,
But we only see in part, like the lunar crescent
Our sight is dimmed by our fear and doubt.
But today we know that Death has been defeated
And the King is on his throne, in peace he's seated.

"Resurrection"

O Lord, please show me your unseeable face,
Even though if I see it I will die.
O take me up into that placeless place,
The celestial rose that forms the celestial eye.
Raise me as you raised your blessed Son,
Let what is dead come forth into new life.
The seed you planted now rises with the sun,
A vine with branches ready for the knife.
Prune back the dead to give new life a way
Of growing in the home you've made for us.
Give us songs to sing and games to play,
For our bodies will be raised out of the dust.
Until that day we with the angels sing,
And rejoice for the coming of our King.

"Re-Creation"

The once-dead Earth is coming back to life,
We see the first fruits rising from the ground.
We hear the music of the birds whose flight
Signals that the land is no longer drowned.
Drinking deep of this life-giving water,
The means of death has caused new life to be;
Life from death and joy comes with it after
Death and decay have gone into the sea.
And the Sun now rises more golden than before,
The Moon and Stars more luminous and bright.
All we have to do is open up the door
And not allow ourselves to fear the night.
For there is one who knocks at the door for us,
And he breathes life into the meanest dust.

"New Life"

Spring winds blow the seeds of resurrection,
Daffodils are bursting from the ground.
Snowdrops and tulips and buds on trees are found
In the morning of the vernal insurrection.
Birds begin their mating communication,
Badger brock begins to stir around,
Squirrels and rabbits dance in the sun and bound
About in a graceful dance of exaltation.
But where is the new life of Spring in me?
How can I find joy in every moment?
And how can I learn to grow into my being?
Make me a new creation, let me see
The part I play in this cosmic movement
So I can be myself at last and sing.

"Christ in Creation"

The risen Word gives rise to the written word
For which the holy monks made illuminations.
They saw viridity in the living earth
And brought to life the Scriptures through creation.
They saw the smoke of mystic incense rising,
And they captured it in their sacred knots.
Their devotion shouldn't be surprising,
They saw with eyes that we have long since lost.
Jesus was found in every brook and stream,
Swimming with dolphins and flying with the birds.
He came to them as though a waking dream,
His voice in every wind and song was heard.
By their love for the risen One,
They saw him in the Moon, the Stars, the Sun.

"Apostles"

The tomb was empty on that Sunday morning
And angels waited for the coming women,
Mary Magdalene and the others mourning
The death of one they thought would lead to heaven,
Wondering how they'd move the massive stone
To lovingly prepare the dead man's body.
These women walked the dusty path alone,
For the men had given him up completely.
Angels told them not to be afraid,
Christ was no longer lying in the tomb.
Death's dominion was at last unmade,
The bride should now prepare for the loving groom.
All this the women reported to the disciples,
And so became apostles to the apostles.

"Pentecost"

At Babel we had our languages confused
Because we thought we could build up to the sky
And pull God down, leaving him to die,
Leaving him in the dust alone, unused
As we took his throne, humanity unloosed,
Unbound and freed from the fetters by which he tried
To control us. The life he offered we thought a lie
And so by our pride, we were cast out like refuse.
But then we committed an even graver sin
And nailed the God who sought us to the cross;
Despite his love, we fed him to our ire.
Yet he refused to leave us in the bin,
He died to give us back what we had lost,
And sent the Spirit of Language like tongues of fire.

Ordinary Time

"Jacob's Ladder"

Ascending and descending the angels fly,
Going about their secret ministrations,
Rejecting as unworthy our adulations,
Showing themselves only to those with eyes
Made clean, to eyes that have been purified.
They work behind the scenes, an undulation
Of hidden waves, of hidden murmurations
We cannot sense no matter how hard we try.
But if you can find the Stone of Destiny,
The rock on which poor Jacob laid his head,
The Stone on which he slept, on which he dreamed,
The Earth will seem as liminality.
It teems with life, it lives and is not dead,
And every single creature is more than it seems.

"The Milky Way"

Herbert said it was a kind of prayer,
The galaxy in which we spin and live.
Looking up, he saw what you had to give,
He saw it through the liminal, luminous air.
For him there was no light-polluted layer
To obscure his sight, which allowed him to believe
That the whole of God's creation is alive
In him and shining with celestial flare.
But I can barely see the stars at night,
Let alone Phaeton's streak across the sky.
So how am I to use it as I pray
When it has been obstructed by our lights?
But then I see the pictures by those who try,
And I can say I've prayed the Milky Way.

"To Strengthen the Heart"

You give us bread to strengthen our weary hearts,
Fruit of the earth and work of human hands.
The staff of life so simply made imparts
A simple joy that's found in every land.
But then you took the humble loaf of bread
Made from water, flour, salt, and yeast
And changed its substance for your Son's, once dead
But now our ever-living, holy high priest.
This bread is more than food, it is our cure,
Giving us strength to make it through the day.
It transfigures us into a people pure,
Able to face the challenges on the way.
In the name of the Father, Son, and Holy Ghost,
This bread becomes for us the blessed Host.

"To Gladden the Heart"

For the Psalmist, wine brings the heart joy,
And it ought to bring us conviviality,
A life that's lived together which employs
This elevating spirit, a modality
Of what the rich and poor can easily share.
This fruit of the vine that's crushed and left to receive
The work of spirits dancing in the air,
They transform the juice into something we can hardly believe,
But then you make it into something more,
Something more than this drink which we call wine.
Just as the water became wine when it was poured,
It now becomes the blood of the divine.
By a different kind of joy we are emboldened
When to our Savior's blood we are beholden.

"The Holy Fool"

His grey and wiry hair falls in tangled knots;
His beard is long and hallows his ancient face.
He wanders the streets and talks and talks and talks,
Wandering the streets without a trace
Of real direction for his stumbling feet.
Then I see him stop in the local park by a tree.
He stops and makes himself a little seat,
So he can watch a passing bumble bee.
He talks to the bee and looks up at the tree and smiles,
Throws back his head and laughs and laughs and laughs.
I watch him closely, staring all the while,
"Why are you laughing?" I get the courage to ask.
"I see the fairies flying with the bees;
I see the angels dancing in the trees."

"Ekstasis"

Poets must be called from death to life,
For the *ekstasis* is certainly a kind of death
Where the Spirit of Creation fills our breath
And cuts us to the quick like an exacting knife.
The Spirit comes like Pan upon his fife,
Playing music through the reeds and in the depths
Of the whispering flames upon the hearth,
Leading us to lands both grim and bright.
But even when we're called back from the edge,
And brought into the world of everyday,
We keep the poet's roving eye and flame
Which glances Heaven through the earthly sludge
And sees the Earth in a transfiguring way,
Giving "airy nothings" a local name.

"Kairos"

For everything there is a time
A season proper for its execution.
But what about this ordinary season of mine,
A monotony without a resolution?
Spinning between the dishes, laundry, work,
I am a top twirling in its place.
And yet I do not stop, I dare not shirk
These mundane duties of mine in a mundane space.
But is there anything that's ordinary,
Anything beneath me, below my station?
Isn't just to be extraordinary,
Even the smallest molecule in creation?
For everything there is its proper season,
And we are ordered by the Divine Reason.

Stations of the Cross

"Station I"

"Take up your cross and follow me," you said.
We couldn't know then exactly what you meant,
But then they placed the thorns upon your head,
And mocked you for their mirthless merriment.
Condemned you did not fight their condemnation,
While they passed you back and forth like a child's game.
Condemned for every person, you are Salvation,
But asking who condemned you, I say my name.
I stood in the crowd and chanted "Crucify!"
I said your blood would be upon my hands.
I drove the nails, I made the Savior cry.
I left the Savior dying, it was my plan.
Condemned you started on your dolorous road,
The cross upon your back your heavy load.

"Station II"

The cross upon your back your heavy load,
You stumble with it on the sinner's way.
Straining with each step upon the road,
Your mouth is shut, you have nothing left to say
Until your final moments on the cross.
What did you think as you started to drink the cup,
The cup you prayed your Father would allow to pass,
The cup that would see you fall and lifted up?
Did you think of those who had abandoned you?
Or the people who desired to watch you die?
Did you think of me and the sinful things I do,
Which led you to the barren hill so high?
Or did you focus on every single breath
As your feet still led you to the death of death?

"Station III"

As your feet still lead you to the death of death,
You stumble on the rocks and stones and holes,
The very rocks you once said could be filled with breath
And cry out your name and move us in our souls.
You fall to show us we can rise again,
That our first fall has now been overcome.
In this fall is our original sin,
And you show us death will one day soon be done.
You fall to the ground, you fall just like a toddler,
Looking for his father, for his mother,
But you fell down to raise up our fallen father,
To loose our first mother from her evil lover.
You lift the cross and rise up to your feet;
You see the woman Eve was meant to be.

"Station IV"

You see the woman Eve was meant to be,
Her heart pierced through by many sorrowful swords.
Her tears obstruct her eyes, she can barely see
As celestial silence sounds from her Son, the Word.
It was her *fiat* that made this possible,
Her "let it be" to undo her mother's "Yes."
But to survive this? it seems impossible,
To see her only Son reduced to less
Than human by our sins and dark cruelty.
And in your eyes, she sees this is not the end,
For in your eyes are comfort and credulity,
Belief that life cannot break, only bend.
But still you bend beneath the heavy cross,
And a man is forced to replace the strength you lost.

"Station V"

A man is forced to replace the strength you've lost,
Simon of Cyrene bears some of the load.
You rise, it is yours to pay the cost,
But Simon remains and joins you on the road.
God has always used his mediators:
Worked through us and not just on his own.
So Simon lifted up our bleeding Savior,
Determined with you to walk, with you to groan.
Would I have taken on my Savior's pain,
Walked with you on the *via dolorosa*?
Or would I have turned my back on you again,
And left you on the path in pain and closer
To the dust from which humanity was made,
With grime and blood and mud upon your face?

"Station VI"

With grime and mud and blood upon your face,
You wander closer to your final hour
When a girl who takes up little space
Proceeds to stop you with her innocent power.
She reaches up to clean you and sees you smile.
You bend down to receive her ministrations.
She delights you for a little while,
And you leave behind the icon of Salvation.
For you are the Image in whose image we are made,
We bear it truly as your bear our sins for us.
But even the Image of God cannot be stayed,
You continue on this path so dolorous.
This brief respite with her can't reel you in,
Your light is flickering out, your beacon's dim.

"Station VII"

Your light is flickering out, your beacon's dim,
And so our God falls down a second time.
This self-kenosis is a weight on him,
The One from Whom all lights receive their shine.
A baby in a manger, so powerless
Is he who made the stars to shine and play.
The Boundless God draws closer to the precipice,
Bounding to his death at the close of day.
Your second fall, your choice of Incarnation
United you to our so fragile flesh.
We'll rise with you, we'll rise in deification,
For with your divinity we have been enmeshed.
But you still have so many miles to go
When you see the Jewish women full of woe.

"Station VIII"

When you see the Jewish women full of woe,
You hear the voice that wept in lamentation,
Rachel's tears and wailing, Rachel brought low,
You see her in their eyes, their consternation.
Another son of Israel struck down,
A servant of the poor oppressed by Rome.
They've lost their hope of freedom, of David's crown
Raising up the tent of Jesse, a new Kingdom.
They didn't know then what you meant to do,
That your enemy was not of flesh and blood.
You came to conquer Death and give us new
Life, a life that's overflowing like a flood.
But before you could destroy Death's vice-like hold,
You had to finish walking up this road.

"Station IX"

You have to finish walking up this road,
To reach the hill, the end for which you were sent.
But the burden wore you down, it brought you low,
And again you fell; the wounds on your back were rent
Open once again, in anticipation
Of the new wounds which you would soon receive,
The holy wounds which would bring us our redemption,
The loving wounds to which we'll forever cleave.
Two times you fell to overcome the past,
But this fall and rising showed to us the future.
Death cannot stand, it cannot even last
A moment in the presence of our Savior.
Up the hill the God-made-man ascended,
But once upon a mountain God descended.

"Station X"

Once upon a mountain, God descended,
When Aaron took up his idolatrous collection.
But when you reached the hill, O Lord, you ascended,
And they disassembled God in strange reflection.
They stripped you of your clothes and left you naked.
They rolled their dice to see who got your tunic.
They thought to leave you exposed, humiliated,
But your divinity could not be wounded.
Fortune seemed to favor those who hurt you,
As they laughed and jeered at you beside the cross.
But fate would show this scene in a different hue
Because you had descended to seek the lost.
Naked they readied you for your execution,
While you were praying for their absolution.

"Station XI"

While you were praying for their absolution,
They nailed you to a cross and raised you up.
They thought this would bring your story to its conclusion;
They didn't know that this was just the next step.
Just like the snake they raised up in the desert,
We look to you on the cross to receive our cure.
The cure you gave to the Israelites was lesser,
For now you wash us clean and make us pure.
Your breathing slows as you're raised, it is nearly over;
The blood begins to pour, you are diminished.
With dying breath you give the Church your Mother,
And then call out at last that it is finished.
The soldier comes with hammer as we tremble in fear,
But he puts the hammer down and takes up the spear.

"Station XII"

He puts the hammer down and takes up the spear
To pierce our Lord right through to his sacred heart.
Blood so red and water falling clear
Pour to the ground and hallow every part.
The Earth becomes the Chalice, the Holy Grail.
It's hallowed by the outpouring of liquid light.
And yet it seems as if you have just failed,
As if, somehow, the darkness has become bright.
But your blood and water soak in and enrich the soil,
And they anoint our first father's forgotten head.
Thus begins the end of pain and toil;
Yet still you hang there, limp and lifeless, dead.
Joseph takes into his hands the holy cup,
And lifts it down, so it can be raised up.

"Station XIII"

Joseph lifts you down so you can be raised up,
Yet everyone believes this is the end.
They think at last that you've run out of luck,
And that they have condolence cards to send.
Mary holds your body in her heart-broken arms;
The sixth sword has stabbed her in the heart.
In this moment, no knowledge can make her warm.
She must feel the sorrow, feel it, every part.
There is no time to properly dress your body,
Prepare it for the end they think you've attained.
You'll be buried peasant-simple, not princely-gawdy.
The women work and the apostles have been shamed.
In hopelessness, I stand outside and groan
As they place you in a tomb that's not your own.

"Station XIV"

They place you in a tomb that's not your own.
The first-born son would never be passed over.
Death has come to bring you to his home,
Little knowing this catch he could not cover.
Old Death will be consumed by what he's eaten.
He's finally caught a life he cannot kill.
But three days would pass before he would be beaten,
And we are left alone in darkness, silence, still.
We're left to wonder if it's worth the cost
To follow you into the dark unknown.
Your light's gone out; without it we are lost.
It feels as though we're walking all alone.
We leave you in the tomb, alone and dead.
"Take up your cross and follow me," you said.

The Planets

"Luna"

In a muddy pool I see your reflection,
The silver rays that wander in the night.
I see you only through refracted light
And something stirs in the back of my recollection.
My mind begins to wander in a new direction
And so I see things with a different sight,
The Holy Fool has always had it right
And so we need some lunatic correction.
Just like the Moon, we wax and wane, we change.
As the light that she receives is transfigured
And she transfigures our ever wandering feet
As our minds her silver light at last invades
And brings us dreams and images and figures
While we make the Stone of Destiny our seat.

"Mercury"

As I ascend through translunatic flight,
I see the Lord of Language and of Meaning.
He shows me not a single word is trite,
And that this foray is only the beginning.
As I consider this, I think with the stars,
And as I breath, the Spirit of the Wind
Blows into my soul, my self, and dares
Me to see that the Heavens are not dimmed
Just because we call them space and sky.
For space is just a place that's filled with Him,
And the sky was once the heavens to our eyes,
While books are the bark of forests wild within.
Yet the Lord of Meaning is mercurial,
He often changes us through our words and wills.

"Venus"

Morning Star, the Apostle Paul's third heaven,
Lady of Love, you show to us real beauty,
You show it to us freely, wholly, truly.
God the Mother, you are the fertile leaven,
You brought the Earth to life within those seven
Days. You gave birth and mythologically
We conceived a way to tell your story,
As you brooded over us, your own dear children.
Even Star, how could we have forgotten,
Forgotten that beauty can deceive us,
Unless it is wed to truth and to the good.
Do not let us be deceived and so besotted,
But as our dearest Lover, please receive us,
And give to us the Love that is our food.

"Sol"

The Sun shines through the ugly window panes,
And on my cheek I feel its womb-like warmth.
This light, it seems to burn away my sins,
And leads me out beyond celestial shores
Where I will find the source of every light,
The Sun who flames itself in three, whose might
Destroys our sins and forgives us of our doubt.
But I am not yet ready to withstand
The full abundance of this solar love
And so I return at his divine command
The Light still shining on me from above.
But now my eyes are burned by cosmic fire
And I can nearly see through mists and mire.

"Mars"

A red light gleams in the sky above, it makes
My blood begin to boil with dreams of courage.
I long for the past, for deeds of a "purer age"
Where I might fight with brother knights and take
The adventure set before me to streams and lakes,
To holy hermits praying in the forest
Where for my food I must search and hunt and forage,
And find my thirst in holy wells well slaked.
But iron swords will take and do not give,
And iron nails once gave us iron cruelty,
So I must beat myself into a plowshare.
Still, I will fight injustices, so others can live,
And I will fight the sins inside of me.
But death? It died when the stranger's tomb was bare.

"Jupiter"

There is a wounded king who travels near,
Whose royal robes of blue swirl in the wind.
He is the King of Summer, no need to fear,
His scabbard is empty, his sword is left behind.
We feast and sing in the halcyon days of his reign,
And in his light I feel magnanimous.
I could dance all night and sing until the day came.
This jovial, jolly King, he makes us joyous.
And while his ancient father lies ahead,
And threatens us with death and with decay,
The King reminds us that Death at last is dead,
That we will live and feast in eternal day.
But his stormy wound still bleeds in ancient rhyme,
And will not heal until the end of time.

"Saturn"

Death, decay, and pestilence all reign
When Time is marching ever forward to
Entropy. The Black Hole of all that once was new
Consumes the Real again and again and again.
He leaves us nothing, nothing but our pain.
As He consumes the stars and mountains, who
Can stand against him, can lead us somewhere new
Where Time does not mean loss but to regain?
But perhaps we do not know this Father Time.
Perhaps his scythe is not to kill, but to harvest,
And perhaps he wants to bring us into the Light.
It is our sin that makes us sick with grime
And only Time can lead us to the furthest
Reaches of the World beyond the night.

Mysteries of the Rosary

Glorious Mysteries

"Resurrection"

A poor man buried in a rich man's tomb behind
A stone so large there are few who could move it.
Guarded by soldiers as though they feared the Wind
Might blow the body away and so remove it.
But on that Sunday morning the angels rolled
The stone to let the Living Man walk out.
Death had made an attack that was too bold,
His forces recoiled like an army in a rout.
Like snow in the Spring, Death's power melted away,
Melted into water that lets the seeds
Once dead now spring to life and blossom and play.
They drink the water and on the Sun they feed.
The Son of Man and Son of God is risen,
And he has made a palace of our prison.

"Ascension"

For forty days the risen Lord went feasting,
Even cooking breakfast for his apostles.
But then the day arrived for his ascending,
And he blessed his friends, his dear disciples.
He had to go prepare a place for us,
A place he will bring at his returning.
Somehow he will, that day, transform our dust
Into a life of infinite enduring.
But we needn't look up to see where he has gone,
For he has gone beyond both time and space.
Instead we must look into our hearts for his throne,
For that is where he made his resting place.
We take him with us throughout the entire world,
And preach the Good News of the living Word.

"Descent"

He ascended to send down the Spirit,
The Paraclete, the Helper for his siblings.
The Hidden Fire descended and appeared
As tongues of flame that set the people trembling.
They breathed in the Spirit then breathed out the Word,
Speaking in the tongues of all the nations
To spread the news of Christ to all the world,
And offer everyone eternal salvation.
So why do I still hide myself away,
Acting like this belongs to someone else?
Lead me through the fear and show me the way
To bring the Truth to others and to myself.
Descend on me, sweet Spirit from above,
And lead me to the final sphere of Love.

"Assumption"

An old woman on her deathbed tells
Her friends and family that they must still love
As they have been taught to do, and swell
Their breath full of grace from the Spirit of God above.
They must not weep as this is not her end;
Her son is coming down to bring her home.
Death will not take our holy Savior's friend,
His loving mother whom he longs to welcome
Body and soul into his blessed kingdom.
And so the Son takes up his mother's hand,
Lifting her from her mortal home and bed,
She ascends into the undying lands
Never being counted among the dead.
Immaculate, she came into and left the world,
The stars placed round her shoulders like a robe unfurled.

"Coronation"

Heaven's holy queen was once a girl
Who lived and breathed in ancient Palestine.
Now she sits enthroned above the world
And champions the stars so they will shine.
Symbol of the world and church exalted,
Sophia crowned with stars and clothed with the Sun,
Standing on the Moon she is undaunted
By the dragon who once tried to eat her Son.
She is the example of the deified
Of the end for which each one of us was made.
Through her Son she left the dragon defied,
But first she was the Lord's humble handmaid.
And before she was crowned the glorious Queen of Heaven,
She rose in humility like bread enleavened.

Joyful Mysteries

"Annunciation"

"Let it be as you have said," the Handmaid
Of the Lord gives her consent. Her *Fiat*
Echoes back to when God eternally brought
The stars, the earth and all that was ever made
Into its bright existence. Through what she said
Mary becomes a kind—though humanly not
Divinely—of co-creatrix; it is her lot
To be the Mother of our Lord and his handmaid.
But we should not forget that Heaven's Queen
Was a young and humble Jewish girl.
She lived and loved and laughed and had her fears.
She walked the streets of Palestine, seen
And heard, and likely suffered insults hurled
At her. This is our Queen, who cried real tears.

"Visitation"

Two pregnant women meet, it is so strange
To think that something so natural could lead
Them to a moment of eternal exchange,
A moment so simple, like the counting of a bead.
And yet it is so oddly extraordinary,
Life makes its home in a woman's womb,
Life which we think so dully ordinary
Is itself a gift, one lost too soon.
But when Mary meets her pregnant, Levite cousin,
One baby in a womb, he leaps for joy
In the presence of the one who undoes sin.
And Elizabeth, she longs for Mary's boy.
Adding to the gift of their conceptions,
Our Savior meets them in this visitation.

"Nativity"

The night is cold when Mary begins to push,
She's giving birth in the strangest circumstances.
For God is not coming in a flaming, unburnt bush,
Even if he comes during cosmic dances.
Recently wed, she seems like just a girl,
Just another Jewish girl who's giving birth.
But this girl was about to change the world.
Because she said yes, the Savior comes to earth.
Surrounded by the animals of labor,
She labored on, pushing even harder,
Delivering up her Son who on Mt. Tabor
Would show himself as God in the human garden.
But Mary knew she'd one day feel the loss
Of seeing her Son dying on the cross.

"Presentation"

Too poor to buy the proper sacrifice,
Mary and Joseph buy two simple doves.
Their Son was the Lamb who'd one day pay the price,
On whom the Dove would descend, the Spirit of Love.
He brought joy to the hearts of Simeon and Anna
While he, the Word, lay cooing, infant-wordless.
They saw before them the living Manna,
The One who came to die, to fight while swordless.
They prophesied the rise and fall of many,
The redemption of eternal Jerusalem,
An old man and woman dreaming dreams of plenty,
Of the baby who at last had come to save them.
Present him to us, sweet Mary, holy mother,
That we may meet humanity's true Lover.

"Finding"

Jesus stayed behind in Jerusalem,
With all the precociousness of a twelve-year-old.
He knew his Father's will could never fail him,
But still, you likely thought he should told
You where he was and not just disappear.
After all, it was you who had been given
The Son of God, he was placed in your care,
And yet it was his work, his job to enliven,
To give us life abundantly, with joy.
What did you think when you saw him sitting down
And all the priests listening to your little boy,
Teaching them before he received his crown?
Did you rejoice to see him at his work?
Could you see the devil waiting where he lurked?

Sorrowful Mysteries

"Agony"

He asked his friends to wait with him a while,
So he could pray before his final hour.
He prayed for us, the lowly rank and file,
But he also prayed that he could be passed over.
Who would want to die upon the cross?
Who so easily would give up their life?
And yet, though he asked for the cup of death to pass
He would not abandon his adulterous wife.
He submitted his human will to the divine,
And sweat with blood before he died for us.
He would give up his life and all to give me mine,
And you yours. He would die for us and still be sinless.
Three times he had to wake his sleeping friends,
And even for them he would have to make amends.

"Scourging"

They tied you to a post and tore your skin,
All so Pilate could finally let you go.
But since it was the Truth he didn't know,
He couldn't keep you from the clamoring din,
The shouts of hate which represent our sin.
Still they whipped you, counting every blow,
Hoping with this gruesome, vulgar show
The cries to end your life would be reined in.
But Pilate could not stop the will of God,
And the evil desired would be turned to good,
And the blood you lost was only the down payment.
For Death was about to swallow too big a Word,
One it could not speak in its evil mood,
Changing Death into a beautiful raiment.

"Coronation"

They crowned you as befits your kingly station;
They put the imperial robe upon your shoulders.
They struck you and you gave no protestation,
And so they hit you harder feeling bolder.
The crown upon you brow is filled with thorns,
Driving always into your aching head.
The crown grows red with blood as it is worn,
And still you are alive and not yet dead.
Stripped again, they leave you with your crown,
Believing with it you are humiliated.
They prepare to march you through the heart of the town,
Not knowing that their sins would be expiated.
You submit yourself to their cruel humility
Because you made us for sublimity.

"Carrying"

They make him carry a gallows on his back;
They make him tie the knot of his own noose.
They thought it was their choice, that he didn't choose
To walk on this death march, on Death's own track.
But in this the crowd and his tormentors lacked
The higher knowledge of just what it was
That Christ had come to do, and yet because
They didn't know, he marched to his final act.
And so he walked the path to trample Death,
Every step a toll to sound the end.
And on his back the means of execution,
Not for him, but for Death's final breath.
He went to die so that he might send
Us to our home, our final resolution.

"Crucifixion"

"Cursed is the man who hangs upon a tree,"
So Moses told the ancient Israelites.
But you were there to be a curse for me,
To bring to an end by your kenotic might
The wages of our sin, our final death.
Not one of us was good enough to die,
Despite our souls breathed in by holy breath,
We were too trapped by sin to even try.
But by the death of God we reached at-one-ment,
Just as at his birth he joined his nature to ours.
But his death was the final, missing component,
Which allowed us to join the celestial choirs.
People watched him die in sullen mood,
But this was the Friday we'd one day soon call good.

Luminous Mysteries

"Baptism"

Water rushed by, the Light of the Sun reflected,
Light, and water, and the descent of the dove,
And a voice, a thunderous voice, which echoed above,
For God had come in form and place unexpected.
He hallowed the waters before he was rejected.
John buried Christ and brought him up resplendent.
The waters changed that day, were filled with love.
He cleansed the waters, which cleanse us and reprove,
He washed the waters on which we are dependent.
Every drink I take, and every time I wash,
The hallowed water enters into my life.
It doesn't matter that I'm made from ash.
He hallowed dust, just as he hallowed strife.
This hallowed water brings me to the hallowing Christ.

"Wedding"

"They're out of wine," his mother said to him.
"Woman, what has that to do with me?"
But water comes again, to make us see.
"Do what he says," as she draws the servants in.
"Draw the water, fill the cups to the brim."
By his desire for festive joy, for free
He gave the gift of wine. Matrimony
And all other celebrations are blessed from within.
So I now sip my glass of red, a cabernet
Or Pinot Noir. And I participate
In that wedding feast, the one which called ahead,
To the paschal feast on that fateful Lenten day.
So I have drunk his blood in wine, and I ate
His flesh under the guise of humble bread.

"Proclamation"

From mountainside, from boats and beaches, the cry
Is heard of Kingdom come, of God among us.
In synagogues, he reads the scrolls about why
The servant came to set the captive, us,
Free. To cheer the poor, raise up the lowly,
And as his Mother said to Elizabeth,
He came to cast down from their throne the mighty.
This was his message, he would not take a breath
Until lifted up he take his last, the final
Breath, these words his final homily:
"Into your hands, I commend my spirit, all
Is done." But we still need help, need eyes to see.
With these words we hear the proclamation
Of Kingdom Come, of hope, of our salvation.

"Transfiguration"

Taboric light, shekinah mist unveils
The Truth, the hidden Light behind the Shadow.
The dull becomes radiant, and holy blows
The wind. The three men continue to tell their tale.
Moses and Elijah prep the Holy Grail.
Peter sees and kneels and bends and bows
While James and John sit silent, Peter knows
Not what to say, his understanding fails.
The Light and mist return from whence they come,
Only to find their way back to the earth.
For Christ and Spirit dwell inside us all,
And he united all things from our home
To his unapproachable divinity, our worth
Refreshed with light and life from one eternal.

"Institution"

He lifts himself when lifting up the bread,
And in the cup of wine they drink his blood.
He presents himself to us just as should
Because he is alive who once was dead.
With the whole of Christ we are wholly fed,
And are consumed by this our holy food.
We become what we eat, and this is good
For we are washed by his flesh and the blood he bled.
But how do I live this all consuming life?
And how is it the substance is transformed?
And how could he join to our humanity?
Consumed I no longer live for sin and strife,
But am transfigured by the one who performed
The final task. I in him and he in me.

Apostles' Creed

"I believe in God, the Father almighty, Creator of heaven and earth"

I am made in the image of the Maker,
The Author and the Poet of our world,
The One who is the only true Creator,
The One who set all galaxies to swirl.
He made the forests with their fungal fronds
Connecting all the roots from tree to tree.
He made the swamps, the oceans, and the ponds
Teeming with life impossible to see.
And then there are the unseen mysteries:
Angels and spirits flocking in the air.
Yes, he made these, the lower divinities
And humankind who would become his heir.
He made all this and more we do not know,
So we can see and learn, create and grow.

"and in Jesus Christ, his only Son, our Lord,"

We can see and learn, create and grow
Because we have been joined to Christ the Son.
He is the Word of the Father, who allows us to know
That God is three and yet also One.
He is the Son, the truly spoken Word,
The Image of the invisible Father.
He is the Word of God that all things heard,
Which spoke them into being ever after.
He is the perfect, only thought of God
The Beloved of the only true Lover.
And yet He is God, his very thought
Eternally begotten of the Father.
He is the image into which we're made,
And it is his Image which we have betrayed.

"who was conceived by the Holy Spirit, born of the Virgin Mary,"

Because it is his Image we have betrayed,
The Son was born again but now in time.
In the virgin-womb of Mary he was laid
By the Spirit's glory, the Spirit's shine.
His mother gave him our humanity
So could he save all that he had assumed
Joining us to his divinity.
He came to kill the beast that had consumed
Every aspect of our daily lives.
Death had haunted us for so long,
And yet he had not made us just to die.
So he was born a baby in the womb,
But he was headed for the stranger's tomb.

"suffered under Pontius Pilate, was crucified, died and was buried;"

He was headed for the stranger's tomb,
Pontius Pilate had made sure of that.
He washed his hands, walked out of the room,
And left him to the Rebel's artless trap.
We put him on the tree so he would die,
It was our sins that pierced him to the heart.
Caught up in the diabolic lies,
We killed the One who loved us from the start.
They buried him quickly, they left the Christ alone.
There was no time for ritual or prayer.
Soldiers blocked him in with a large stone
And closed the door on the Father's only heir.
They guarded him, but what they didn't know,
Is He had another journey still to go.

"he descended into hell; on the third day he rose again from the dead;"

Christ had another journey still to go,
He crashed the gates of Hell and knocked them down.
He preached his victory, the final blow
Which left the devil defeated and on the ground.
He rescued some, the ones who were meant for heaven,
While Death was left to contemplate his loss.
Everything was planned, success a given,
The game was over when God was on the cross.
But the tomb was opened up three days later,
The Righteous One came strolling from the grave.
Death had lost its sting to a force that's greater,
The force of Divine Life who'd come to save.
On that Sunday morning everything was new.
New life had fallen on us like the morning dew.

"he ascended into heaven, and is seated at the right hand of God the Father almighty;"

New life has fallen on us like the morning dew,
But Christ no longer walks the streets with us.
He said he had some other work to do
With the Father to prepare for us.
Forty days he stayed but then ascended,
Promising to send the Paraclete.
When he returns Death will be upended,
But until then, like friends, with Death we'll meet
And journey onward to the One who sits
At the right hand of the Father on his throne.
Our temporary, soulish, bodiless visit
Is just the beginning, for Christ's work is not done.
But until then we'll have to wait and pray
For Christ's return on that triumphant day.

"from there he will come to judge the living and the dead."

For Christ's return on that triumphant day
Means judgment for the living and the dead.
When he returns there will be those who say,
"When did we find you hungry and leave you fed?"
When I arrive will I turn to the right,
Counted among the Shepherd's holy sheep?
Or will I turn to the left and lose my sight,
Damned with the demons to that sleepless sleep?
What will I say when faced with what I've done?
And what will I hear when I see his face?
Will he say to me, "Thy will be done?"
Or "Come, my servant, sit in a higher place"?
I take these questions with me into prayer,
And feel the Spirit's breeze blow through the air.

"I believe in the Holy Spirit,"

I feel the Spirit's breeze blow through the air,
The breath that God once used to fill our lungs.
He is the one who groans for me in prayer,
Calling to us, he wants to give us welcome,
To exhort and guide us to the holy life.
He is the Love that's shared between the Beloved
And the Lover, the Gift that's shared with the wife
Of the Son, the tongues of flame, the Dove
That descended on the God-made-man.
He is the mystery we can't quite see,
And he is one with the Father and the Son,
The voice that calls us out beyond the sea.
The Wind of God always blows where it will,
But to hear it we must be quiet and still.

"the holy catholic Church,
the communion of saints,"

And so to hear we must be quiet and still,
The voice of God is ringing in the Church,
The Church that's particular and universal.
And to find its members we haven't far to search.
For we are a Church of the living and the dead,
Of all who've called upon Lord Jesus' Name.
And we are joined by faith, by wine and bread,
And by the Wild Spirit we cannot tame.
We gather at the table, sit down to feast,
Joined by a great cloud of witnesses,
Seated where the humble and the least
Become our masters and our mistresses.
We take the Cup of Glory, drink it in,
We drink together in the Holy Inn.

"the forgiveness of sins,"

We drink together in the Holy Inn,
The saint and sinner sit across the table
Because no matter the terrible weight of sin
The Risen Christ has finally made us able
To break the chains the fallen one has wrought,
The chains that kept us from turning to the Lord.
For by his death, Jesus Christ has bought
Us back from the pretender king and lord.
So now at last we can be forgiven,
There is no wound so large he cannot heal.
We turn to him so we can be shriven,
And once confessed we eat the holy meal.
He heals our souls and bodies so one day
We can be raised up to him and play.

"the resurrection of the body,"

We can be raised up to him and play
Because he didn't come just to save our souls
But saved our bodies too, so on that day
When he comes again to make us whole,
Our dust shall be reformed and be made new.
For what our Lord assumed he also healed,
And like the seed that died we'll grow too,
But what we'll be has not yet been revealed.
We know that Jesus walked out of the grave;
He ate the fish and showed his holy scars.
He showed us we are not just simply saved,
But joined to him in life beyond the stars.
And then we'll finally be free from sinning
At the end which is really the beginning.

"and life everlasting."

At the end which is really the beginning
We'll finally meet our Savior face to face.
And while the stars are re-made in their spinning,
He'll lift us up by his abundant grace.
We'll finally have eyes that see and ears
That hear the finer music of the angels,
The song we call the Music of the Spheres,
The music we couldn't hear when we were entangled.
Oh and we'll sing too in that new life,
We'll make new things we've never dreamed before
Because we'll have become his holy wife,
Further in and up forevermore.
Until then I will write for my Creator,
For I am made in the Image of a Maker.

Benediction

"Ite Missa Est"

Go forth! For now this book is at an end.
Let us give thanks for what we have received.
I pray that I have been God's faithful friend,
And give my work to the God I have believed.
We must receive the Gift and understand
That we are sent to the world, to rocks and trees
And birds and fish and animals on land.
We must go out and take the Gospel Story,
Of God-made-man who died and rose for us,
Defeating Death by death and bringing Glory,
The Holy Spirit who makes our lives more porous.
Go forth! For now this book is at an end
And find the garden you were called to tend.